50 Best of Chili Dishes

By: Kelly Johnson

Table of Contents

- Classic Texas Chili
- Spicy Beef and Bean Chili
- White Chicken Chili
- Vegetarian Three-Bean Chili
- Slow Cooker Pulled Pork Chili
- Green Chili Pork Stew
- Cincinnati Chili
- Black Bean and Sweet Potato Chili
- Turkey Pumpkin Chili
- Chorizo and Black Bean Chili
- Chili con Carne
- Buffalo Chicken Chili
- Beer Braised Beef Chili
- Keto No-Bean Chili
- Chipotle Beef and Corn Chili
- Smoky Bacon and Beef Chili
- Chocolate Mole Chili
- Hatch Green Chile Stew
- Jamaican Jerk Chili
- BBQ Brisket Chili
- Fire-Roasted Tomato Chili
- Spicy Venison Chili
- Thai Red Curry Chili
- Mexican Pozole Chili
- White Bean and Sausage Chili
- Southwest Quinoa Chili
- Ghost Pepper Chili
- Pumpkin and Black Bean Chili
- Brazilian Feijoada Chili
- Bourbon Maple Chili
- Spicy Lamb and Lentil Chili
- Korean Kimchi Chili
- Smoked Brisket Chili
- Peanut Butter and Beef Chili
- Moroccan Spiced Chili

- Italian Sausage and Cannellini Chili
- Honey Chipotle Chicken Chili
- Cajun Gumbo-Style Chili
- Caribbean Coconut Chili
- Maple Bacon Sweet Chili
- Roasted Poblano and Turkey Chili
- Mole-Style Chocolate Chili
- Cornbread Topped Chili Casserole
- Cheesy Chili Mac
- Spicy Shrimp and Chorizo Chili
- Roasted Garlic and Herb Chili
- Bison and Black Bean Chili
- Hatch Chile and Hominy Chili
- Beer and Bratwurst Chili
- Texas Roadhouse Steak Chili

Classic Texas Chili

Ingredients:

- 2 lbs beef chuck, cut into ½-inch cubes
- 2 tbsp vegetable oil
- 1 large onion, diced
- 4 cloves garlic, minced
- 3 tbsp chili powder
- 1 tbsp ground cumin
- 1 tsp smoked paprika
- 1 tsp dried oregano
- ½ tsp cayenne pepper (optional)
- 2 tbsp tomato paste
- 1 cup beef broth
- 1 (14 oz) can crushed tomatoes
- 1 (12 oz) bottle dark beer (optional)
- 1 tbsp apple cider vinegar
- Salt and black pepper to taste

Instructions:

1. Heat oil in a large pot over medium-high heat. Brown beef in batches, then set aside.
2. In the same pot, sauté onions until soft, then add garlic and cook for 1 minute.
3. Stir in chili powder, cumin, paprika, oregano, and cayenne. Cook for 30 seconds.
4. Add tomato paste, stir, then return beef to the pot.
5. Pour in beef broth, crushed tomatoes, and beer. Bring to a boil, then reduce heat.
6. Simmer uncovered for 1.5–2 hours, stirring occasionally.
7. Stir in vinegar, season with salt and pepper, and cook for another 5 minutes.
8. Serve hot with toppings of choice.

Spicy Beef and Bean Chili

Ingredients:

- 2 lbs ground beef
- 1 tbsp vegetable oil
- 1 large onion, diced
- 3 cloves garlic, minced
- 2 tbsp chili powder
- 1 tbsp cumin
- 1 tsp smoked paprika
- ½ tsp cayenne pepper
- 1 (14 oz) can diced tomatoes
- 1 (14 oz) can kidney beans, drained
- 1 (14 oz) can black beans, drained
- 1 cup beef broth
- Salt and pepper to taste

Instructions:

1. Heat oil in a pot over medium heat, then brown the beef.
2. Add onions and garlic, cooking until soft.
3. Stir in chili powder, cumin, paprika, and cayenne.
4. Pour in tomatoes, beans, and broth.
5. Simmer for 30 minutes, stirring occasionally.
6. Season to taste and serve hot.

White Chicken Chili

Ingredients:

- 1 lb shredded cooked chicken
- 1 tbsp olive oil
- 1 small onion, diced
- 3 cloves garlic, minced
- 1 (4 oz) can green chilies
- 1 tsp cumin
- ½ tsp oregano
- ¼ tsp cayenne pepper
- 1 (14 oz) can white beans, drained
- 3 cups chicken broth
- ½ cup heavy cream
- Juice of 1 lime
- Salt and pepper to taste

Instructions:

1. Heat oil in a pot and sauté onion and garlic.
2. Stir in green chilies, cumin, oregano, and cayenne.
3. Add beans, broth, and chicken; simmer for 20 minutes.
4. Stir in cream and lime juice.
5. Season and serve warm.

Vegetarian Three-Bean Chili

Ingredients:

- 1 tbsp olive oil
- 1 large onion, diced
- 3 cloves garlic, minced
- 1 red bell pepper, diced
- 1 (14 oz) can black beans, drained
- 1 (14 oz) can kidney beans, drained
- 1 (14 oz) can pinto beans, drained
- 1 (14 oz) can diced tomatoes
- 1 cup vegetable broth
- 2 tbsp chili powder
- 1 tsp cumin
- ½ tsp smoked paprika
- Salt and pepper to taste

Instructions:

1. Heat oil in a pot and sauté onion, garlic, and bell pepper.
2. Stir in chili powder, cumin, and paprika.
3. Add beans, tomatoes, and broth.
4. Simmer for 30 minutes, stirring occasionally.
5. Season and serve.

Slow Cooker Pulled Pork Chili

Ingredients:

- 2 lbs pork shoulder, cut into chunks
- 1 tbsp olive oil
- 1 large onion, diced
- 3 cloves garlic, minced
- 1 (14 oz) can diced tomatoes
- 1 (14 oz) can black beans, drained
- 1 (14 oz) can kidney beans, drained
- 1 cup beef broth
- 2 tbsp chili powder
- 1 tsp cumin
- ½ tsp smoked paprika
- Salt and pepper to taste

Instructions:

1. Heat oil in a pan and brown pork on all sides.
2. Transfer to a slow cooker with all other ingredients.
3. Cook on low for 6–8 hours or until pork is tender.
4. Shred pork and mix well.
5. Serve warm.

Green Chili Pork Stew

Ingredients:

- 2 lbs pork shoulder, cubed
- 1 tbsp olive oil
- 1 onion, diced
- 3 cloves garlic, minced
- 2 (4 oz) cans diced green chilies
- 1 cup tomatillo salsa
- 3 cups chicken broth
- 1 tsp cumin
- ½ tsp oregano
- Salt and pepper to taste

Instructions:

1. Brown pork in oil over medium heat.
2. Add onion and garlic, cooking until soft.
3. Stir in green chilies, tomatillo salsa, broth, and spices.
4. Simmer for 1.5–2 hours until pork is tender.
5. Serve warm.

Cincinnati Chili

Ingredients:

- 2 lbs ground beef
- 1 tbsp olive oil
- 1 onion, diced
- 3 cloves garlic, minced
- 2 tbsp chili powder
- 1 tbsp cocoa powder
- 1 tsp cinnamon
- ½ tsp allspice
- 1 (14 oz) can tomato sauce
- 2 cups beef broth
- 1 tbsp Worcestershire sauce
- Salt and pepper to taste

Instructions:

1. Brown beef in oil, then add onion and garlic.
2. Stir in spices, then add tomato sauce, broth, and Worcestershire.
3. Simmer for 1 hour, stirring occasionally.
4. Serve over spaghetti with cheese.

Black Bean and Sweet Potato Chili

Ingredients:

- 1 tbsp olive oil
- 1 onion, diced
- 2 cloves garlic, minced
- 1 large sweet potato, diced
- 1 (14 oz) can black beans, drained
- 1 (14 oz) can diced tomatoes
- 2 cups vegetable broth
- 1 tsp cumin
- ½ tsp smoked paprika
- Salt and pepper to taste

Instructions:

1. Heat oil and sauté onion and garlic.
2. Add sweet potato and cook for 5 minutes.
3. Stir in beans, tomatoes, broth, and spices.
4. Simmer for 30 minutes until sweet potatoes are tender.
5. Serve warm.

Turkey Pumpkin Chili

Ingredients:

- 1 lb ground turkey
- 1 tbsp olive oil
- 1 onion, diced
- 2 cloves garlic, minced
- 1 (14 oz) can pumpkin puree
- 1 (14 oz) can diced tomatoes
- 1 (14 oz) can black beans, drained
- 2 cups chicken broth
- 1 tsp cumin
- ½ tsp cinnamon
- Salt and pepper to taste

Instructions:

1. Brown turkey in oil, then add onion and garlic.
2. Stir in pumpkin, tomatoes, beans, broth, and spices.
3. Simmer for 30 minutes, stirring occasionally.
4. Serve warm.

Chorizo and Black Bean Chili

Ingredients:

- 1 lb chorizo, casings removed
- 1 tbsp olive oil
- 1 onion, diced
- 3 cloves garlic, minced
- 1 (14 oz) can black beans, drained
- 1 (14 oz) can diced tomatoes
- 2 cups beef broth
- 1 tsp cumin
- ½ tsp smoked paprika

Instructions:

1. Brown chorizo in oil, then add onion and garlic.
2. Stir in beans, tomatoes, broth, and spices.
3. Simmer for 30 minutes.
4. Serve warm.

Chili con Carne

Ingredients:

- 2 lbs beef chuck, cubed
- 1 tbsp olive oil
- 1 onion, diced
- 3 cloves garlic, minced
- 2 tbsp chili powder
- 1 tsp cumin
- 1 (14 oz) can diced tomatoes
- 2 cups beef broth
- Salt and pepper to taste

Instructions:

1. Brown beef in oil, then add onion and garlic.
2. Stir in chili powder, cumin, tomatoes, and broth.
3. Simmer for 1.5–2 hours until beef is tender.
4. Serve warm.

Buffalo Chicken Chili

Ingredients:

- 1 lb shredded cooked chicken
- 1 tbsp olive oil
- 1 onion, diced
- 2 cloves garlic, minced
- 1 (14 oz) can diced tomatoes
- 2 cups chicken broth
- ¼ cup buffalo sauce
- 1 (14 oz) can white beans, drained
- ½ tsp cumin

Instructions:

1. Sauté onion and garlic in oil.
2. Stir in tomatoes, broth, buffalo sauce, beans, and cumin.
3. Add shredded chicken and simmer for 20 minutes.
4. Serve warm.

Beer Braised Beef Chili

Ingredients:

- 2 lbs beef chuck, cubed
- 1 tbsp olive oil
- 1 onion, diced
- 3 cloves garlic, minced
- 1 (12 oz) bottle dark beer
- 1 (14 oz) can diced tomatoes
- 2 cups beef broth
- 2 tbsp chili powder
- 1 tsp cumin
- Salt and pepper to taste

Instructions:

1. Brown beef in oil, then add onion and garlic.
2. Pour in beer, tomatoes, broth, and spices.
3. Simmer for 1.5–2 hours until beef is tender.
4. Serve warm.

Keto No-Bean Chili

Ingredients:

- 2 lbs ground beef
- 1 tbsp olive oil
- 1 onion, diced
- 3 cloves garlic, minced
- 2 tbsp chili powder
- 1 tsp cumin
- 1 (14 oz) can diced tomatoes
- 1 cup beef broth
- ½ tsp smoked paprika

Instructions:

1. Brown beef in oil, then add onion and garlic.
2. Stir in chili powder, cumin, tomatoes, broth, and paprika.
3. Simmer for 30 minutes.
4. Serve warm.

Chipotle Beef and Corn Chili

Ingredients:

- 1 lb ground beef
- 1 tbsp olive oil
- 1 onion, diced
- 2 cloves garlic, minced
- 1 chipotle pepper in adobo, chopped
- 1 (14 oz) can diced tomatoes
- 1 cup corn kernels
- 2 cups beef broth
- 1 tsp cumin

Instructions:

1. Brown beef in oil, then add onion and garlic.
2. Stir in chipotle pepper, tomatoes, corn, broth, and cumin.
3. Simmer for 30 minutes.
4. Serve warm.

Smoky Bacon and Beef Chili

Ingredients:

- 1 lb ground beef
- 4 slices bacon, chopped
- 1 onion, diced
- 3 cloves garlic, minced
- 1 (14 oz) can diced tomatoes
- 1 (14 oz) can kidney beans, drained
- 2 cups beef broth
- 1 tbsp chili powder
- 1 tsp smoked paprika

Instructions:

1. Cook bacon until crispy, then set aside.
2. Brown beef in bacon drippings, then add onion and garlic.
3. Stir in tomatoes, beans, broth, chili powder, and paprika.
4. Simmer for 30 minutes.
5. Stir in bacon before serving.

Chocolate Mole Chili

Ingredients:

- 2 lbs ground beef
- 1 tbsp olive oil
- 1 onion, diced
- 3 cloves garlic, minced
- 2 tbsp chili powder
- 1 tsp cumin
- 1 tbsp cocoa powder
- ½ tsp cinnamon
- 1 (14 oz) can diced tomatoes
- 2 cups beef broth
- 1 tbsp peanut butter
- ½ oz dark chocolate, chopped

Instructions:

1. Brown beef in oil, then add onion and garlic.
2. Stir in chili powder, cumin, cocoa, and cinnamon.
3. Add tomatoes, broth, peanut butter, and chocolate.
4. Simmer for 30 minutes and serve warm.

Hatch Green Chile Stew

Ingredients:

- 2 lbs pork shoulder, cubed
- 1 tbsp olive oil
- 1 onion, diced
- 3 cloves garlic, minced
- 1 cup roasted Hatch green chilies, chopped
- 3 cups chicken broth
- 1 cup diced potatoes
- 1 tsp cumin
- Salt and pepper to taste

Instructions:

1. Brown pork in oil, then add onion and garlic.
2. Stir in green chilies, broth, potatoes, and spices.
3. Simmer for 1.5–2 hours until pork is tender.
4. Serve warm.

Jamaican Jerk Chili

Ingredients:

- 1 lb ground turkey
- 1 tbsp olive oil
- 1 onion, diced
- 2 cloves garlic, minced
- 1 tbsp jerk seasoning
- 1 (14 oz) can black beans, drained
- 1 (14 oz) can diced tomatoes
- 2 cups chicken broth
- 1 cup chopped pineapple

Instructions:

1. Brown turkey in oil, then add onion and garlic.
2. Stir in jerk seasoning, beans, tomatoes, broth, and pineapple.
3. Simmer for 30 minutes.
4. Serve warm.

BBQ Brisket Chili

Ingredients:

- 2 lbs smoked brisket, chopped
- 1 tbsp olive oil
- 1 onion, diced
- 3 cloves garlic, minced
- 1 (14 oz) can diced tomatoes
- 1 cup BBQ sauce
- 2 cups beef broth
- 1 (14 oz) can kidney beans, drained
- 1 tsp smoked paprika

Instructions:

1. Sauté onion and garlic in oil.
2. Stir in brisket, tomatoes, BBQ sauce, broth, beans, and spices.
3. Simmer for 30 minutes.
4. Serve warm.

Fire-Roasted Tomato Chili

Ingredients:

- 1 lb ground beef
- 1 tbsp olive oil
- 1 onion, diced
- 3 cloves garlic, minced
- 1 (14 oz) can fire-roasted diced tomatoes
- 1 (14 oz) can kidney beans, drained
- 2 cups beef broth
- 2 tbsp chili powder
- 1 tsp cumin

Instructions:

1. Brown beef in oil, then add onion and garlic.
2. Stir in tomatoes, beans, broth, and spices.
3. Simmer for 30 minutes.
4. Serve warm.

Spicy Venison Chili

Ingredients:

- 2 lbs ground venison
- 1 tbsp olive oil
- 1 onion, diced
- 3 cloves garlic, minced
- 2 tbsp chili powder
- 1 tsp cumin
- 1 (14 oz) can diced tomatoes
- 1 (14 oz) can black beans, drained
- 2 cups beef broth

Instructions:

1. Brown venison in oil, then add onion and garlic.
2. Stir in chili powder, cumin, tomatoes, beans, and broth.
3. Simmer for 30 minutes.
4. Serve warm.

Thai Red Curry Chili

Ingredients:

- 1 lb ground chicken
- 1 tbsp coconut oil
- 1 onion, diced
- 2 cloves garlic, minced
- 1 tbsp red curry paste
- 1 (14 oz) can coconut milk
- 2 cups chicken broth
- 1 (14 oz) can chickpeas, drained
- 1 cup diced sweet potatoes

Instructions:

1. Brown chicken in coconut oil, then add onion and garlic.
2. Stir in curry paste, coconut milk, broth, chickpeas, and sweet potatoes.
3. Simmer for 30 minutes.
4. Serve warm.

Mexican Pozole Chili

Ingredients:

- 1 lb ground pork
- 1 tbsp olive oil
- 1 onion, diced
- 3 cloves garlic, minced
- 1 (14 oz) can hominy, drained
- 1 (14 oz) can diced tomatoes
- 2 cups chicken broth
- 1 tsp cumin
- 1 tsp oregano

Instructions:

1. Brown pork in oil, then add onion and garlic.
2. Stir in hominy, tomatoes, broth, and spices.
3. Simmer for 30 minutes.
4. Serve warm.

White Bean and Sausage Chili

Ingredients:

- 1 lb Italian sausage, crumbled
- 1 tbsp olive oil
- 1 onion, diced
- 2 cloves garlic, minced
- 1 (14 oz) can white beans, drained
- 1 (14 oz) can diced tomatoes
- 2 cups chicken broth
- 1 tsp oregano

Instructions:

1. Brown sausage in oil, then add onion and garlic.
2. Stir in beans, tomatoes, broth, and oregano.
3. Simmer for 30 minutes.
4. Serve warm.

Southwest Quinoa Chili

Ingredients:

- 1 cup quinoa, rinsed
- 1 tbsp olive oil
- 1 onion, diced
- 2 cloves garlic, minced
- 1 (14 oz) can black beans, drained
- 1 (14 oz) can diced tomatoes
- 1 cup corn kernels
- 2 cups vegetable broth
- 1 tsp cumin

Instructions:

1. Sauté onion and garlic in oil.
2. Stir in quinoa, beans, tomatoes, corn, broth, and spices.
3. Simmer for 25 minutes until quinoa is tender.
4. Serve warm.

Ghost Pepper Chili

Ingredients:

- 2 lbs ground beef
- 1 tbsp vegetable oil
- 1 onion, diced
- 3 cloves garlic, minced
- 1 ghost pepper, finely chopped (use gloves)
- 2 tbsp chili powder
- 1 tsp cumin
- 1 (14 oz) can diced tomatoes
- 2 cups beef broth
- 1 (14 oz) can kidney beans, drained

Instructions:

1. Brown beef in oil, then add onion and garlic.
2. Stir in ghost pepper, chili powder, cumin, tomatoes, broth, and beans.
3. Simmer for 30 minutes.
4. Serve with caution!

Pumpkin and Black Bean Chili

Ingredients:

- 1 lb ground turkey
- 1 tbsp olive oil
- 1 onion, diced
- 2 cloves garlic, minced
- 1 (14 oz) can black beans, drained
- 1 (14 oz) can diced tomatoes
- 1 cup pumpkin puree
- 2 cups vegetable broth
- 1 tsp cumin

Instructions:

1. Brown turkey in oil, then add onion and garlic.
2. Stir in beans, tomatoes, pumpkin, broth, and cumin.
3. Simmer for 30 minutes.
4. Serve warm.

Brazilian Feijoada Chili

Ingredients:

- 1 lb smoked sausage, sliced
- 1 lb pork shoulder, cubed
- 1 tbsp olive oil
- 1 onion, diced
- 3 cloves garlic, minced
- 1 (14 oz) can black beans, drained
- 1 (14 oz) can diced tomatoes
- 2 cups beef broth
- 1 tsp smoked paprika

Instructions:

1. Brown pork in oil, then add sausage, onion, and garlic.
2. Stir in beans, tomatoes, broth, and paprika.
3. Simmer for 1.5 hours.
4. Serve warm.

Bourbon Maple Chili

Ingredients:

- 2 lbs ground beef
- 1 tbsp olive oil
- 1 onion, diced
- 3 cloves garlic, minced
- ¼ cup bourbon
- 2 tbsp maple syrup
- 1 (14 oz) can diced tomatoes
- 2 cups beef broth
- 1 (14 oz) can kidney beans, drained

Instructions:

1. Brown beef in oil, then add onion and garlic.
2. Stir in bourbon, syrup, tomatoes, broth, and beans.
3. Simmer for 30 minutes.
4. Serve warm.

Spicy Lamb and Lentil Chili

Ingredients:

- 1 lb ground lamb
- 1 tbsp olive oil
- 1 onion, diced
- 3 cloves garlic, minced
- 1 cup lentils
- 1 (14 oz) can diced tomatoes
- 2 cups beef broth
- 1 tsp cumin
- ½ tsp cayenne pepper

Instructions:

1. Brown lamb in oil, then add onion and garlic.
2. Stir in lentils, tomatoes, broth, and spices.
3. Simmer for 40 minutes.
4. Serve warm.

Korean Kimchi Chili

Ingredients:

- 1 lb ground pork
- 1 tbsp sesame oil
- 1 onion, diced
- 2 cloves garlic, minced
- 1 cup kimchi, chopped
- 1 (14 oz) can diced tomatoes
- 2 cups chicken broth
- 1 tbsp gochujang

Instructions:

1. Brown pork in oil, then add onion and garlic.
2. Stir in kimchi, tomatoes, broth, and gochujang.
3. Simmer for 30 minutes.
4. Serve warm.

Smoked Brisket Chili

Ingredients:

- 2 lbs smoked brisket, chopped
- 1 tbsp olive oil
- 1 onion, diced
- 3 cloves garlic, minced
- 1 (14 oz) can diced tomatoes
- 1 cup beef broth
- 1 cup BBQ sauce
- 1 (14 oz) can kidney beans, drained

Instructions:

1. Sauté onion and garlic in oil.
2. Stir in brisket, tomatoes, broth, BBQ sauce, and beans.
3. Simmer for 30 minutes.
4. Serve warm.

Peanut Butter and Beef Chili

Ingredients:

- 2 lbs ground beef
- 1 tbsp olive oil
- 1 onion, diced
- 3 cloves garlic, minced
- 2 tbsp peanut butter
- 1 (14 oz) can diced tomatoes
- 2 cups beef broth
- 1 (14 oz) can kidney beans, drained

Instructions:

1. Brown beef in oil, then add onion and garlic.
2. Stir in peanut butter, tomatoes, broth, and beans.
3. Simmer for 30 minutes.
4. Serve warm.

Moroccan Spiced Chili

Ingredients:

- 1 lb ground lamb
- 1 tbsp olive oil
- 1 onion, diced
- 3 cloves garlic, minced
- 1 tsp cumin
- ½ tsp cinnamon
- 1 (14 oz) can chickpeas, drained
- 1 (14 oz) can diced tomatoes
- 2 cups beef broth

Instructions:

1. Brown lamb in oil, then add onion and garlic.
2. Stir in cumin, cinnamon, chickpeas, tomatoes, and broth.
3. Simmer for 30 minutes.
4. Serve warm.

Italian Sausage and Cannellini Chili

Ingredients:

- 1 lb Italian sausage, crumbled
- 1 tbsp olive oil
- 1 onion, diced
- 2 cloves garlic, minced
- 1 (14 oz) can cannellini beans, drained
- 1 (14 oz) can diced tomatoes
- 2 cups chicken broth
- 1 tsp oregano

Instructions:

1. Brown sausage in oil, then add onion and garlic.
2. Stir in beans, tomatoes, broth, and oregano.
3. Simmer for 30 minutes.
4. Serve warm.

Honey Chipotle Chicken Chili

Ingredients:

- 1 lb shredded chicken
- 1 tbsp olive oil
- 1 onion, diced
- 2 cloves garlic, minced
- 1 chipotle pepper in adobo, chopped
- 1 tbsp honey
- 1 (14 oz) can diced tomatoes
- 2 cups chicken broth
- 1 (14 oz) can black beans, drained

Instructions:

1. Sauté onion and garlic in oil.
2. Stir in chicken, chipotle, honey, tomatoes, broth, and beans.
3. Simmer for 30 minutes.
4. Serve warm.

Cajun Gumbo-Style Chili

Ingredients:

- 1 lb andouille sausage, sliced
- 1 tbsp olive oil
- 1 onion, diced
- 2 cloves garlic, minced
- 1 (14 oz) can diced tomatoes
- 2 cups chicken broth
- 1 cup okra, sliced
- 1 tsp Cajun seasoning

Instructions:

1. Brown sausage in oil, then add onion and garlic.
2. Stir in tomatoes, broth, okra, and Cajun seasoning.
3. Simmer for 30 minutes.
4. Serve warm.

Caribbean Coconut Chili

Ingredients:

- 1 lb ground turkey
- 1 tbsp coconut oil
- 1 onion, diced
- 2 cloves garlic, minced
- 1 (14 oz) can coconut milk
- 2 cups chicken broth
- 1 (14 oz) can black beans, drained
- 1 tsp curry powder

Instructions:

1. Brown turkey in coconut oil, then add onion and garlic.
2. Stir in coconut milk, broth, beans, and curry powder.
3. Simmer for 30 minutes.
4. Serve warm.

Maple Bacon Sweet Chili

Ingredients:

- 1 lb ground beef
- 4 slices bacon, chopped
- 1 tbsp olive oil
- 1 onion, diced
- 3 cloves garlic, minced
- 2 tbsp maple syrup
- 1 (14 oz) can diced tomatoes
- 2 cups beef broth
- 1 (14 oz) can kidney beans, drained
- 1 tsp chili powder

Instructions:

1. Cook bacon in oil until crispy, then set aside.
2. Brown ground beef in the same pan, then add onion and garlic.
3. Stir in maple syrup, tomatoes, broth, beans, and chili powder.
4. Simmer for 30 minutes.
5. Stir in bacon before serving.

Roasted Poblano and Turkey Chili

Ingredients:

- 1 lb ground turkey
- 2 poblano peppers, roasted and chopped
- 1 tbsp olive oil
- 1 onion, diced
- 3 cloves garlic, minced
- 1 (14 oz) can diced tomatoes
- 2 cups chicken broth
- 1 tsp cumin
- Salt and pepper to taste

Instructions:

1. Roast poblano peppers, then chop them.
2. Brown turkey in oil, then add onion and garlic.
3. Stir in poblano peppers, tomatoes, broth, cumin, salt, and pepper.
4. Simmer for 30 minutes.
5. Serve warm.

Mole-Style Chocolate Chili

Ingredients:

- 2 lbs ground beef
- 1 tbsp olive oil
- 1 onion, diced
- 3 cloves garlic, minced
- 2 tbsp chili powder
- 1 tbsp cocoa powder
- 1 tbsp peanut butter
- 1 (14 oz) can diced tomatoes
- 2 cups beef broth
- 1 oz dark chocolate, chopped

Instructions:

1. Brown beef in oil, then add onion and garlic.
2. Stir in chili powder, cocoa, and peanut butter.
3. Add tomatoes, broth, and chocolate.
4. Simmer for 30 minutes.
5. Serve warm.

Cornbread Topped Chili Casserole

Ingredients:

- 2 lbs ground beef
- 1 tbsp olive oil
- 1 onion, diced
- 3 cloves garlic, minced
- 1 (14 oz) can diced tomatoes
- 2 cups beef broth
- 1 (14 oz) can kidney beans, drained
- 1 batch cornbread batter (prepared)

Instructions:

1. Brown beef in oil, then add onion and garlic.
2. Stir in tomatoes, broth, and beans.
3. Simmer for 30 minutes.
4. Pour chili mixture into a casserole dish, top with cornbread batter.
5. Bake at 375°F for 25-30 minutes.
6. Serve warm.

Cheesy Chili Mac

Ingredients:

- 1 lb ground beef
- 1 tbsp olive oil
- 1 onion, diced
- 3 cloves garlic, minced
- 2 tbsp chili powder
- 1 (14 oz) can diced tomatoes
- 1 (14 oz) can kidney beans, drained
- 2 cups beef broth
- 2 cups elbow macaroni, cooked
- 2 cups shredded cheddar cheese

Instructions:

1. Brown beef in oil, then add onion and garlic.
2. Stir in chili powder, tomatoes, beans, and broth.
3. Simmer for 30 minutes.
4. Stir in cooked macaroni and cheese.
5. Serve warm.

Spicy Shrimp and Chorizo Chili

Ingredients:

- 1 lb chorizo, sliced
- 1 lb shrimp, peeled and deveined
- 1 tbsp olive oil
- 1 onion, diced
- 3 cloves garlic, minced
- 1 (14 oz) can diced tomatoes
- 2 cups chicken broth
- 1 tsp smoked paprika
- ½ tsp cayenne pepper

Instructions:

1. Cook chorizo in oil, then set aside.
2. Sauté shrimp in the same pan, then set aside.
3. Sauté onion and garlic, then stir in tomatoes, broth, paprika, and cayenne.
4. Return chorizo and shrimp to the pot.
5. Simmer for 15 minutes.
6. Serve warm.

Roasted Garlic and Herb Chili

Ingredients:

- 2 lbs ground beef
- 1 tbsp olive oil
- 1 onion, diced
- 3 cloves garlic, roasted and mashed
- 1 (14 oz) can diced tomatoes
- 2 cups beef broth
- 1 tbsp Italian seasoning
- 1 tsp smoked paprika

Instructions:

1. Brown beef in oil, then add onion and garlic.
2. Stir in roasted garlic, tomatoes, broth, Italian seasoning, and paprika.
3. Simmer for 30 minutes.
4. Serve warm.

Bison and Black Bean Chili

Ingredients:

- 2 lbs ground bison
- 1 tbsp olive oil
- 1 onion, diced
- 3 cloves garlic, minced
- 1 (14 oz) can black beans, drained
- 1 (14 oz) can diced tomatoes
- 2 cups beef broth
- 1 tsp cumin

Instructions:

1. Brown bison in oil, then add onion and garlic.
2. Stir in beans, tomatoes, broth, and cumin.
3. Simmer for 30 minutes.
4. Serve warm.

Hatch Chile and Hominy Chili

Ingredients:

- 2 lbs ground pork
- 1 tbsp olive oil
- 1 onion, diced
- 3 cloves garlic, minced
- 2 Hatch chiles, roasted and chopped
- 1 (14 oz) can hominy, drained
- 1 (14 oz) can diced tomatoes
- 2 cups chicken broth

Instructions:

1. Brown pork in oil, then add onion and garlic.
2. Stir in Hatch chiles, hominy, tomatoes, and broth.
3. Simmer for 30 minutes.
4. Serve warm.

Beer and Bratwurst Chili

Ingredients:

- 4 bratwurst sausages, sliced
- 1 tbsp olive oil
- 1 onion, diced
- 3 cloves garlic, minced
- 1 (14 oz) can diced tomatoes
- 2 cups beef broth
- 1 (12 oz) bottle beer
- 1 tsp caraway seeds

Instructions:

1. Cook bratwurst in oil, then set aside.
2. Sauté onion and garlic in the same pan, then stir in tomatoes, broth, beer, and caraway seeds.
3. Add bratwurst back to the pot.
4. Simmer for 30 minutes.
5. Serve warm.

Texas Roadhouse Steak Chili

Ingredients:

- 2 lbs beef sirloin, cubed
- 1 tbsp olive oil
- 1 onion, diced
- 3 cloves garlic, minced
- 2 tbsp chili powder
- 1 tsp cumin
- 1 (14 oz) can diced tomatoes
- 2 cups beef broth
- 1 (14 oz) can kidney beans, drained

Instructions:

1. Brown beef in oil, then add onion and garlic.
2. Stir in chili powder, cumin, tomatoes, broth, and beans.
3. Simmer for 30 minutes.
4. Serve warm.

www.ingramcontent.com/pod-product-compliance
Lightning Source LLC
LaVergne TN
LVHW081331060526
838201LV00055B/2580